Arpeggio Studies

in Two Octaves

for the Cello

by Cassia Harvey

CHP155

©2011 by C. Harvey Publications All Rights Reserved.
6403 N. 6th Street
Philadelphia, PA 19126
www.charveypublications.com

First Study

Cassia Harvey

©2010 C. Harvey Publications All Rights Reserved.

Arpeggio Studies in Two Octaves for Cello

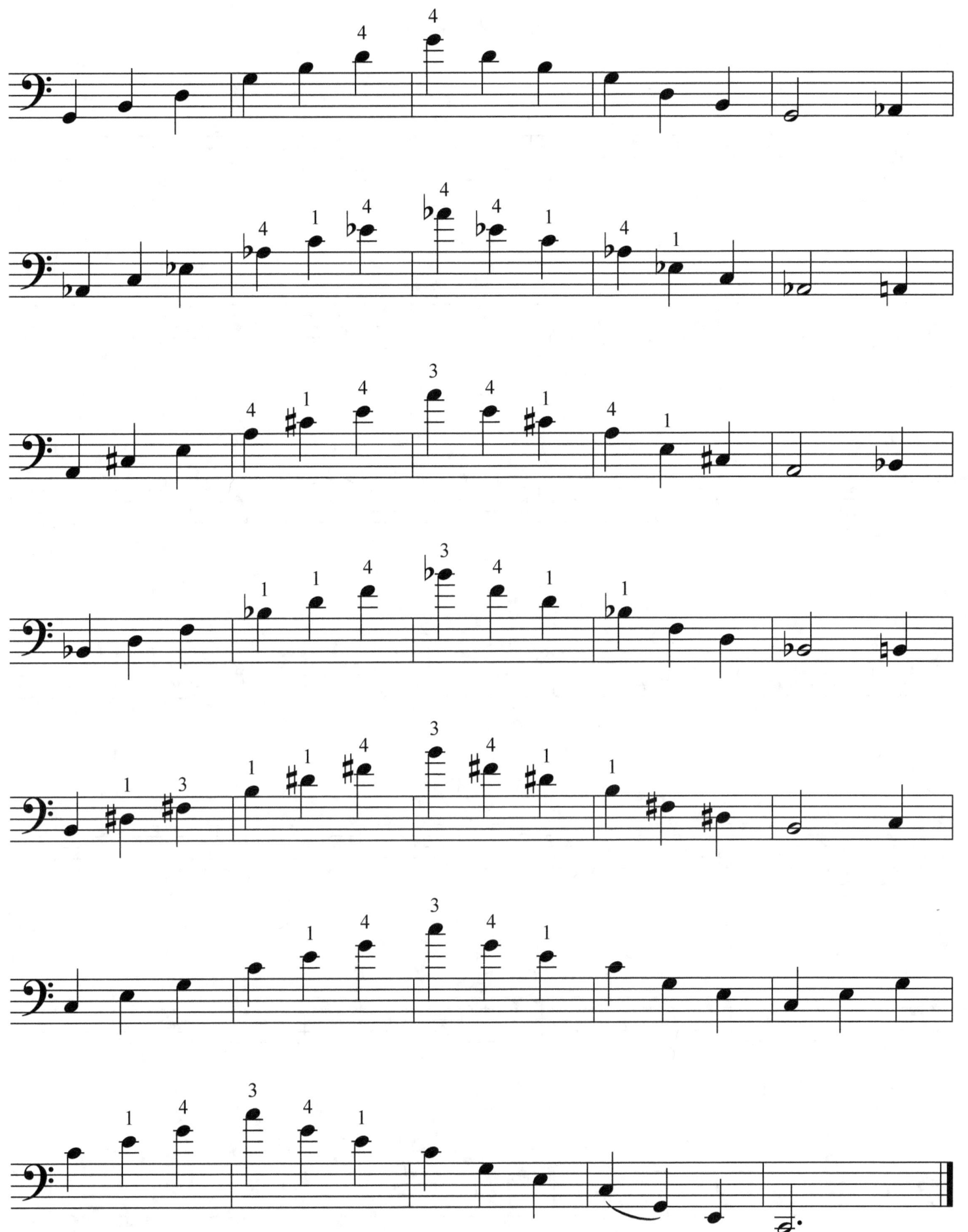

©2010 C. Harvey Publications All Rights Reserved.

Second Study

Arpeggio Studies in Two Octaves for Cello

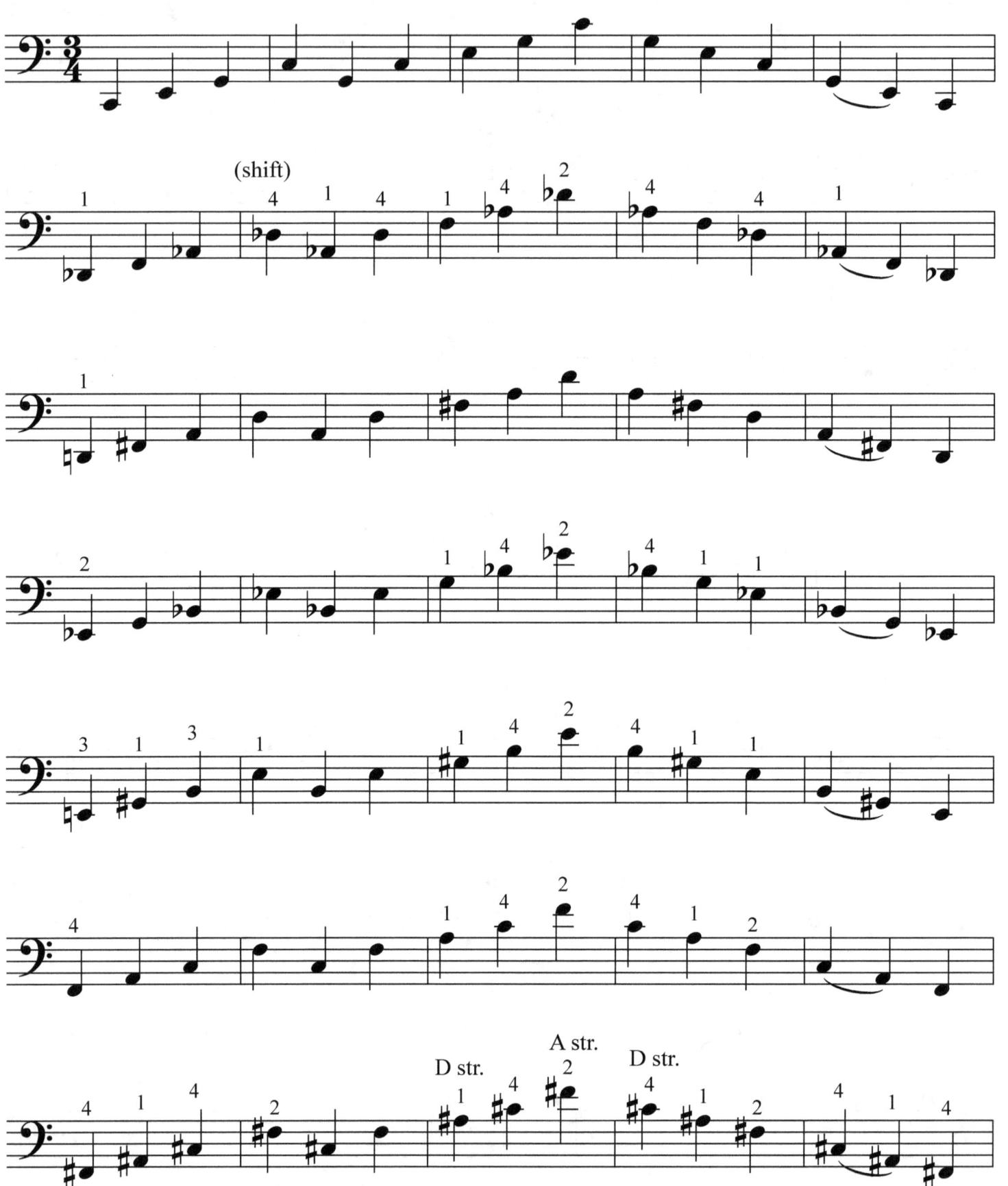

©2010 C. Harvey Publications All Rights Reserved.

Arpeggio Studies in Two Octaves for Cello

Third Study

Arpeggio Studies in Two Octaves for Cello

©2010 C. Harvey Publications All Rights Reserved.

Arpeggio Studies in Two Octaves for Cello

Fourth Study

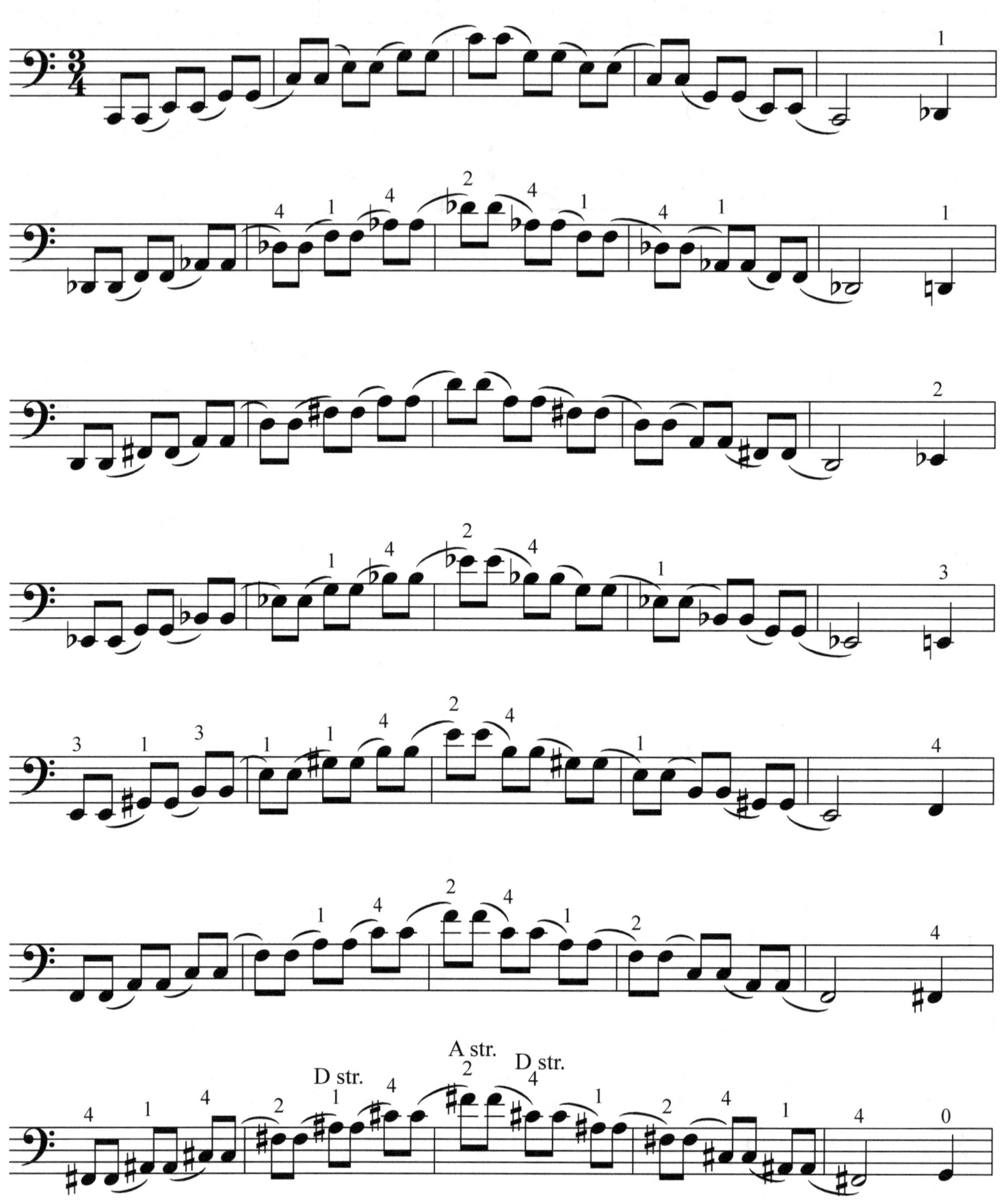

Arpeggio Studies in Two Octaves for Cello

Fifth Study

Arpeggio Studies in Two Octaves for Cello

©2010 C. Harvey Publications All Rights Reserved.

Arpeggio Studies in Two Octaves for Cello

©2010 C. Harvey Publications All Rights Reserved.

Sixth Study

Arpeggio Studies in Two Octaves for Cello

©2010 C. Harvey Publications All Rights Reserved.

Arpeggio Studies in Two Octaves for Cello

Seventh Study

Arpeggio Studies in Two Octaves for Cello

©2010 C. Harvey Publications All Rights Reserved.

Arpeggio Studies in Two Octaves for Cello

Eighth Study

Arpeggio Studies in Two Octaves for Cello

17

Ninth Study

Arpeggio Studies in Two Octaves for Cello

19

Tenth Study

Arpeggio Studies in Two Octaves for Cello

©2010 C. Harvey Publications All Rights Reserved.

Arpeggio Studies in Two Octaves for Cello

©2010 C. Harvey Publications All Rights Reserved.

Eleventh Study

Arpeggio Studies in Two Octaves for Cello

23

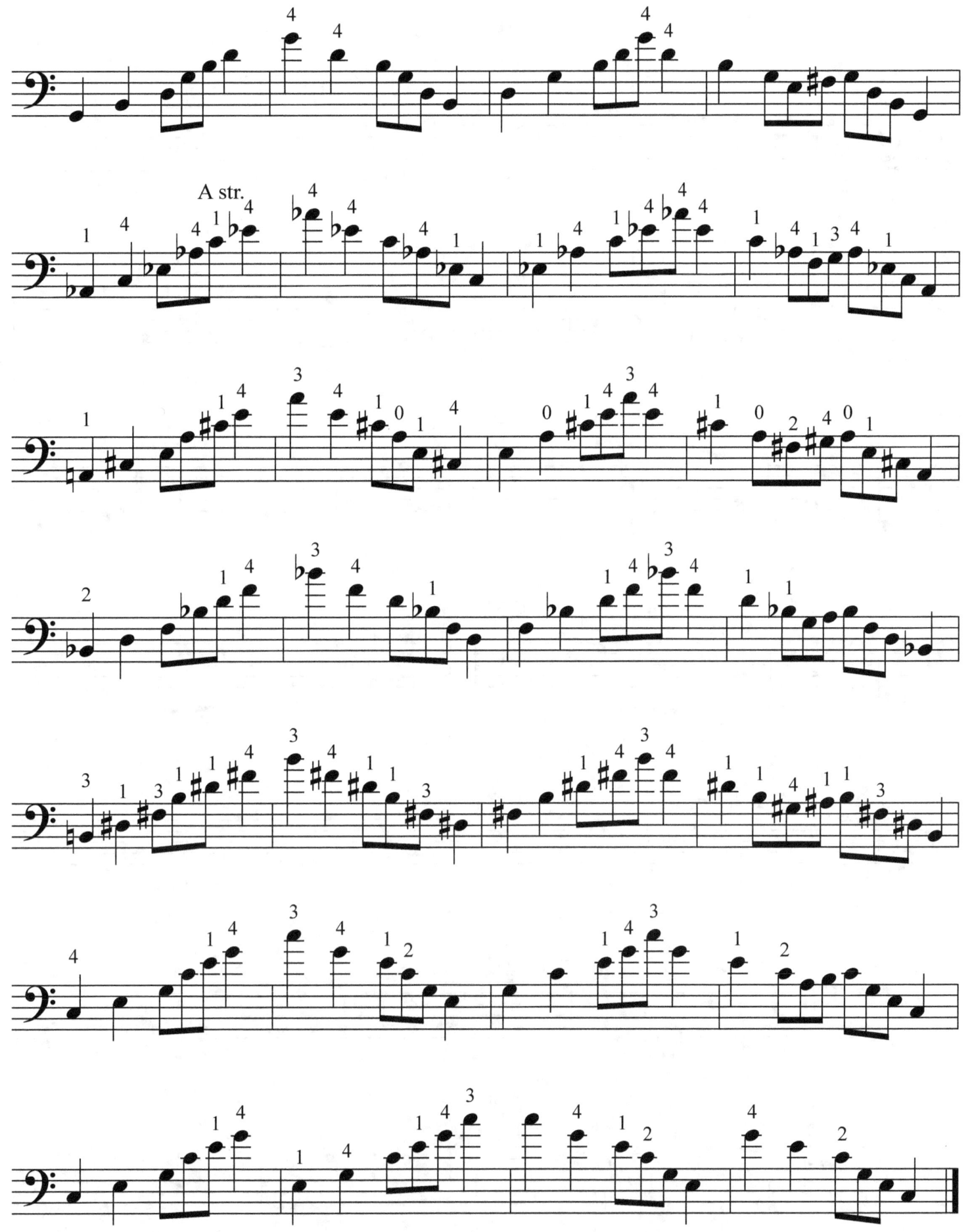

©2010 C. Harvey Publications All Rights Reserved.

Twelfth Study

Arpeggio Studies in Two Octaves for Cello

25

©2010 C. Harvey Publications All Rights Reserved.

Thirteenth Study

Arpeggio Studies in Two Octaves for Cello

©2010 C. Harvey Publications All Rights Reserved.

Fourteenth Study

Arpeggio Studies in Two Octaves for Cello

Fifteenth Study

Arpeggio Studies in Two Octaves for Cello

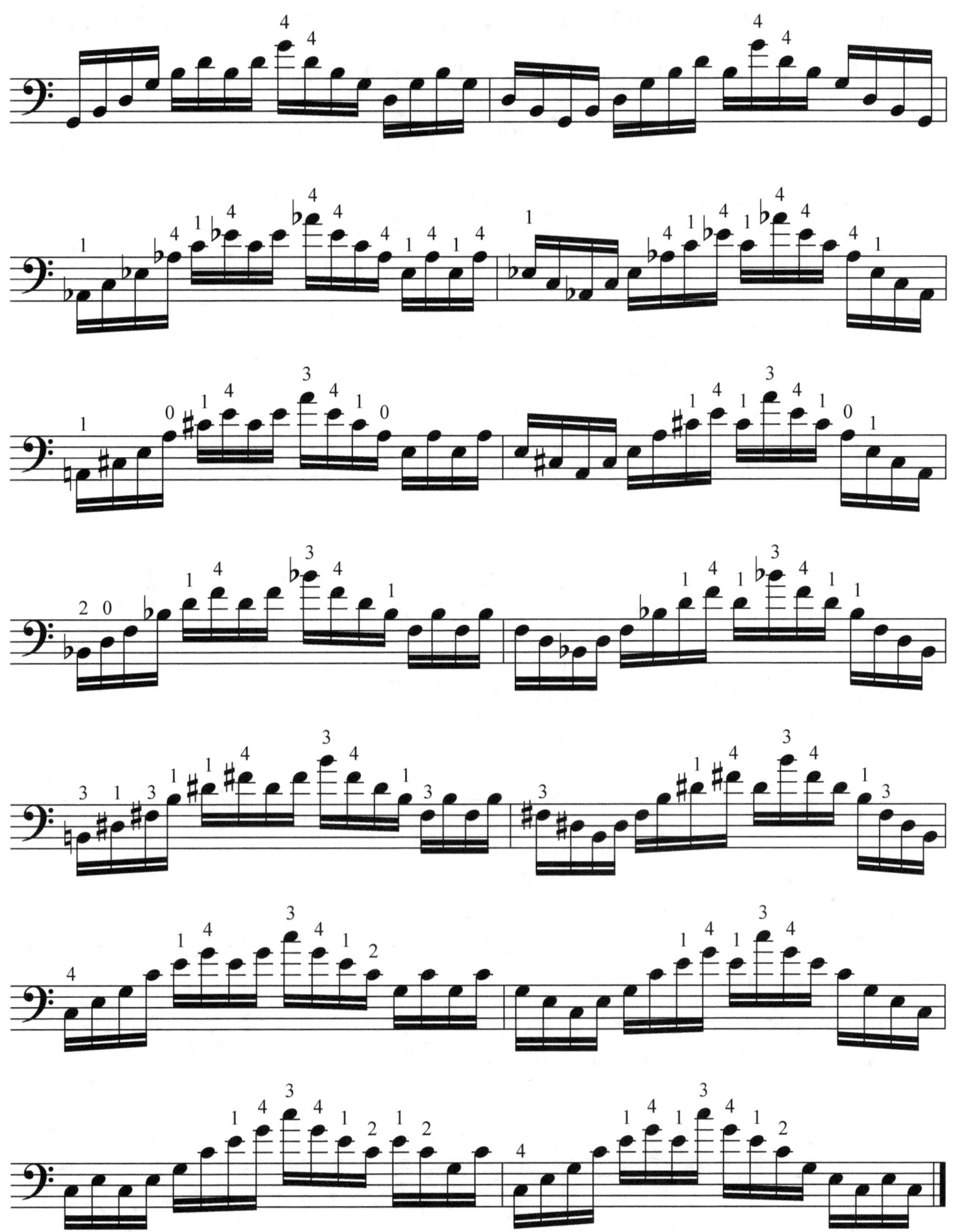

available from www.charveypublications.com: CHP244

Shifting in Keys for Cello, Book One

C Major Study No. 1

©2014 C. Harvey Publications All Rights Reserved.

www.ingramcontent.com/pod-product-compliance
Lightning Source LLC
Chambersburg PA
CBHW051430070526
44584CB00023B/3654